HUGGYSWEET
COZY CHRISTMAS
CUTE and COMFY Coloring Book

This coloring book invites you to a sweet and relaxing experience. Take your markers and color these cute and joyful illustrations on the theme of Christmas with sweet and fun scenes. Sit back and enjoy moments of relaxation to let your creativity run wild!

Published in 2024 by "HUGGYSWEET" edition

BEFORE YOU START
Amazon's paper is great for coloring with colored pencils and alcohol-based markers. Use a blank sheet behind the page for wet media to avoid bleed-through.

CUTE AND COMFY COLORING BOOK
visit our instagram account @HUGGYSWEET

Huggysweet

THIS BOOK
BELONGS TO

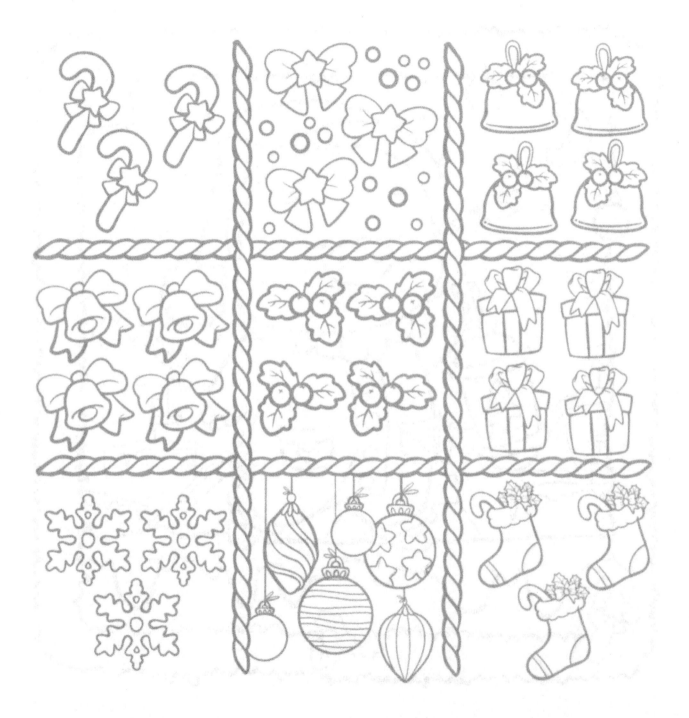

FLOUR

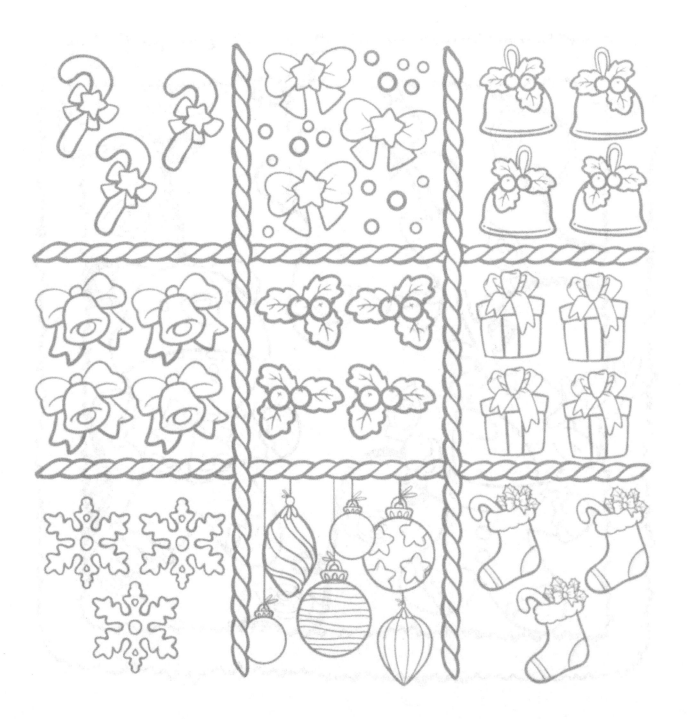

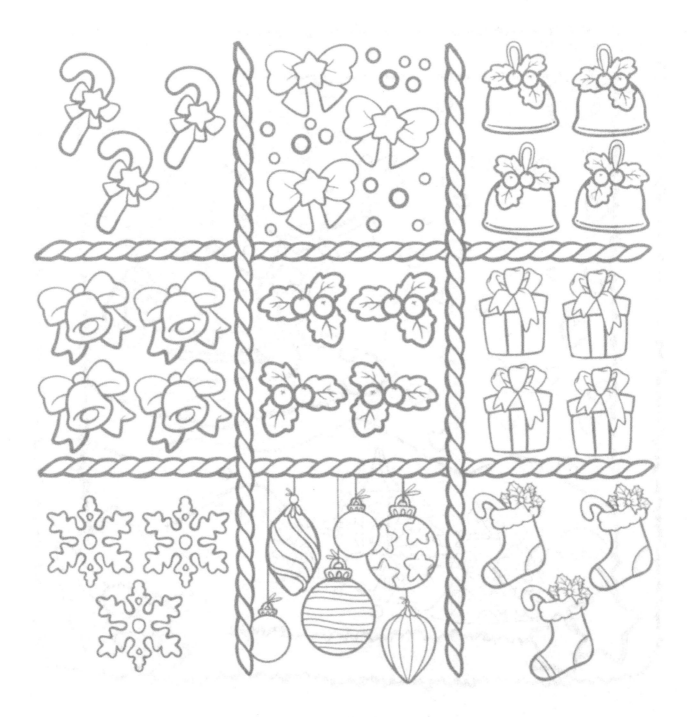

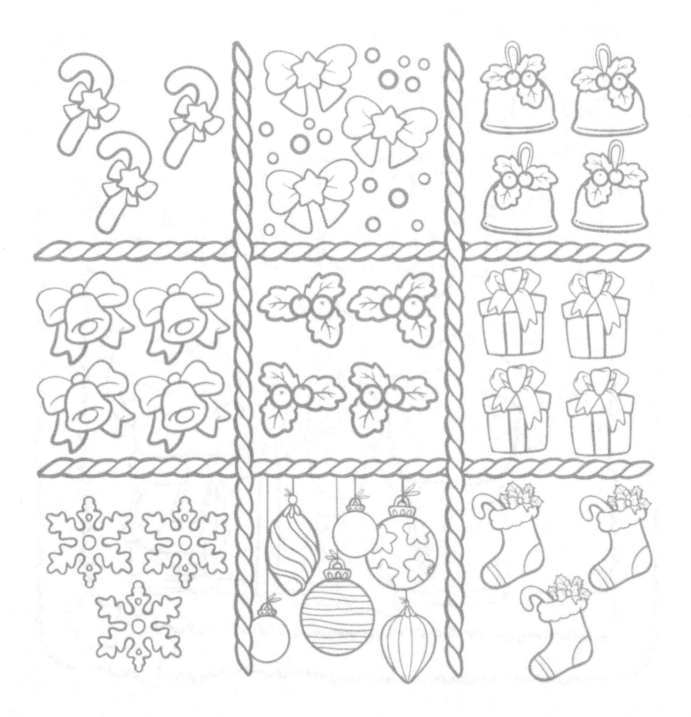

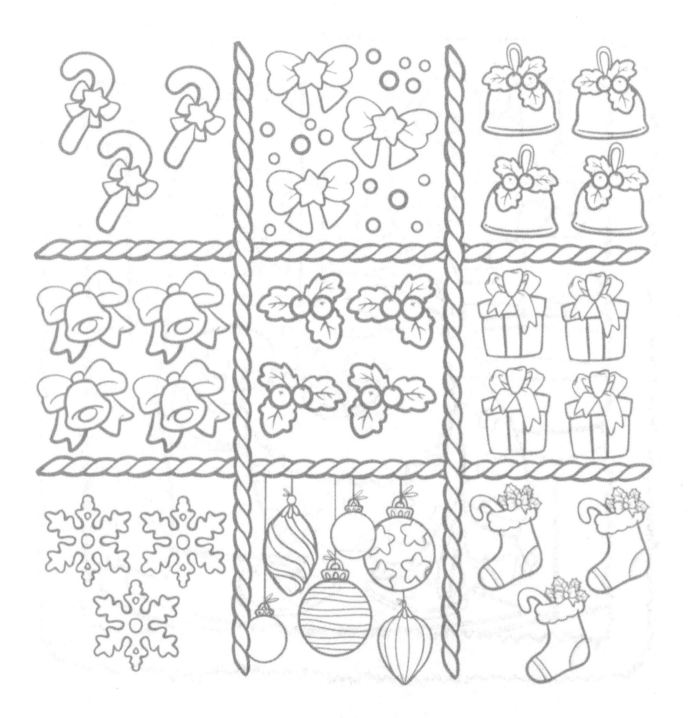

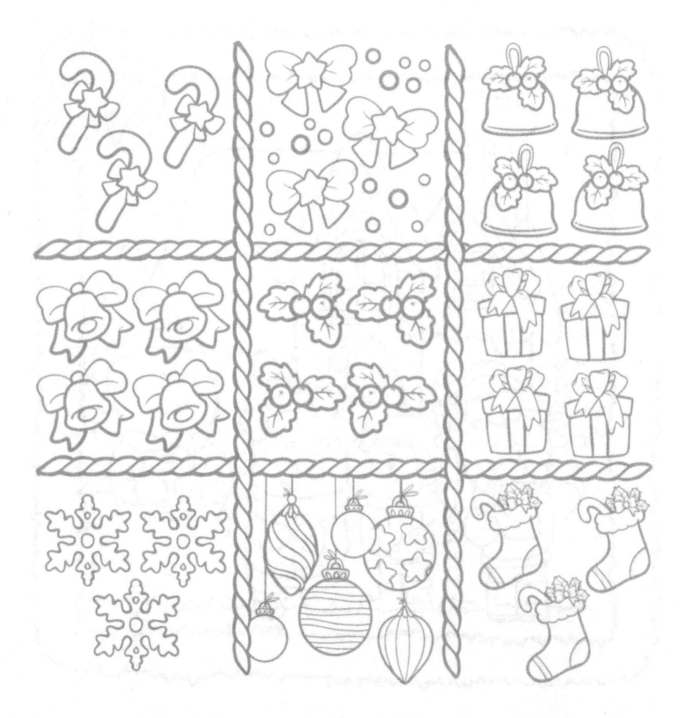

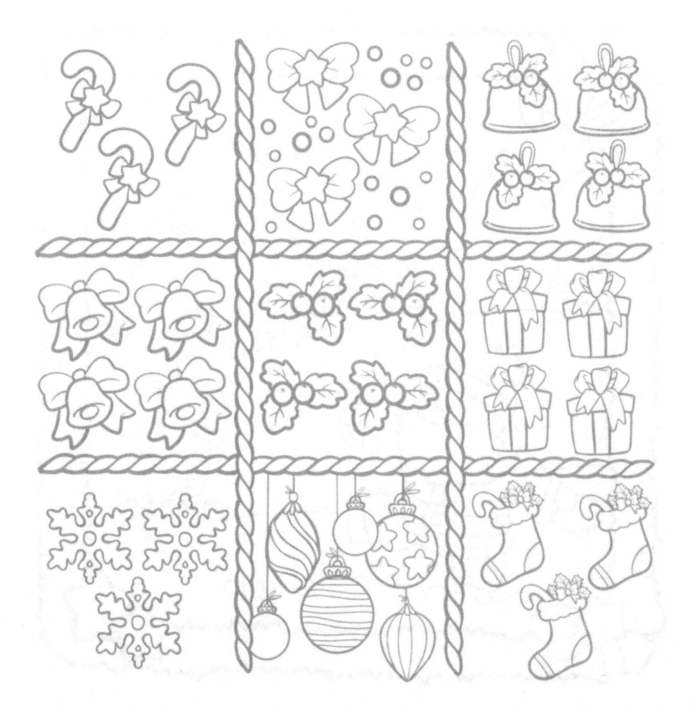

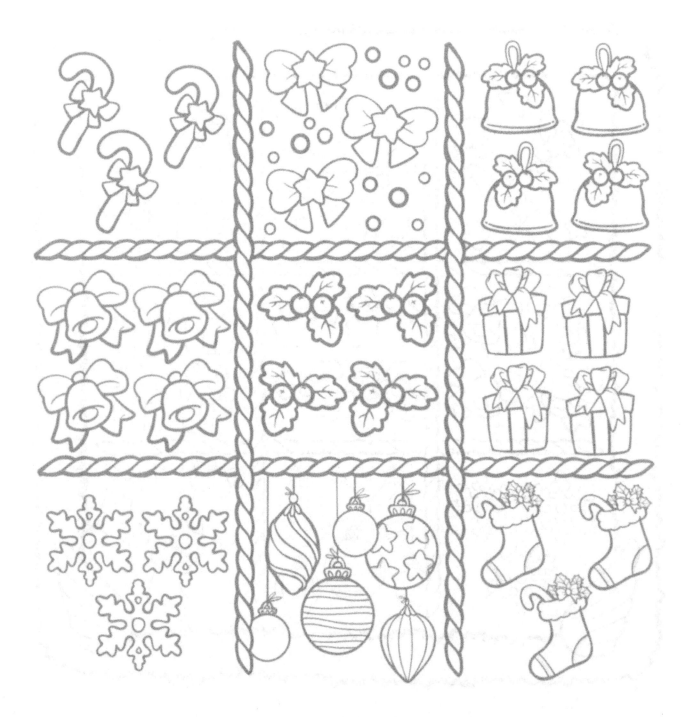

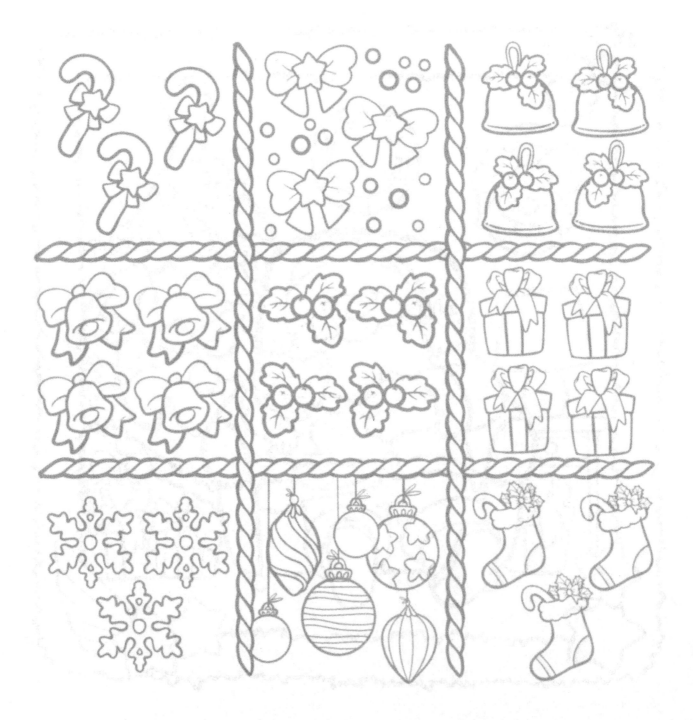

Made in the USA
Las Vegas, NV
22 November 2024

12403837R00050